THE EAST LANCASHIRE RAILWAY

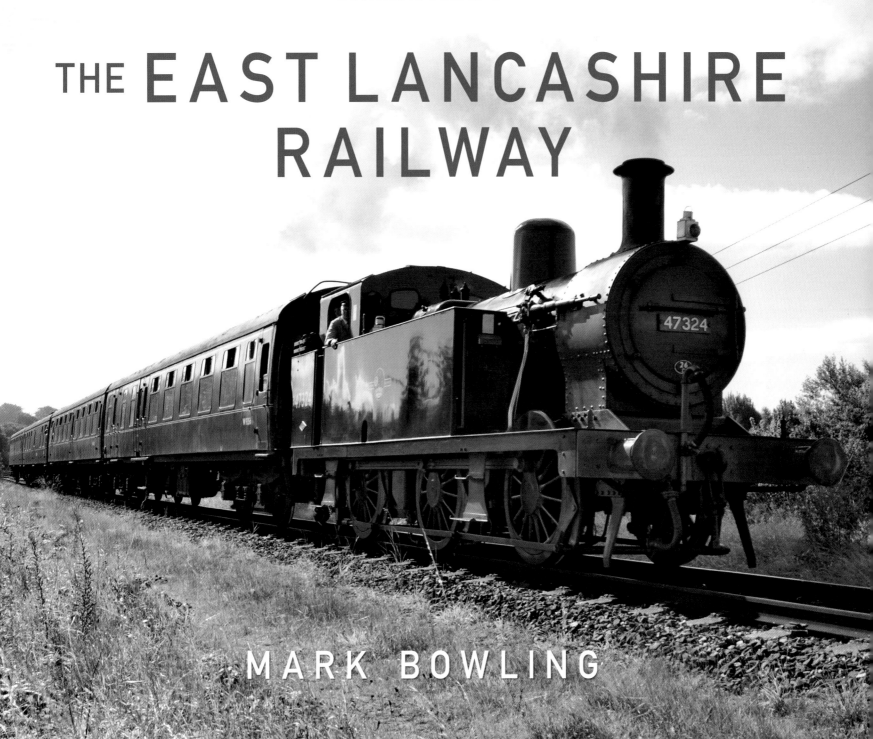

Amberley

THE EAST LANCASHIRE RAILWAY

MARK BOWLING

First published 2011

Amberley Publishing
The Hill, Stroud,
Gloucestershire, GL5 4EP

www.amberleybooks.com

British Library Cataloguing in Publication Data.
A catalogue record for this book is available from the British Library.

ISBN 978-1-4456-0519-7

Typesetting and Origination by Amberley Publishing.
Printed in Great Britain.

INTRODUCTION

The East Lancashire Railway is a relative newcomer to the preserved railways of Great Britain. Despite this, it has quickly grown into a major tourist attraction. Direct main-line access and generous curves mean that the railway regularly runs visiting stock, including the largest main-line locomotives from all four pre-grouping regions.

In 1984, the East Lancashire Railway Trust was formed. This was a partnership between the East Lancashire Railway Society and the two local authorities, their aim being to restore, re-open, operate and maintain the railway. Success came in July 1987 when the first four miles between Bury and Ramsbottom were opened to passengers.

Further success followed with the new station buildings at Ramsbottom being opened in 1989. A new terminus station was constructed at Rawtenstall, and in April 1991 the section of line between Ramsbottom and Rawtenstall was opened. This extended the line to eight miles, with three stations plus two intermediate halts at Summerseat and Irwell Vale.

The extension to Heywood, vital for main-line access, proved to be the most problematical, with major engineering works and much legislation to be overcome. Embankments, new bridges, track laying and re-signalling were all eventually completed and new legislation relating to Railway Privatisation was met. Finally, in September 2003, this section of line was opened to regular passenger services.

The line runs through a diverse landscape, including towns, industrial areas and large rural sections. The railway has numerous river crossings, passes through cuttings and tunnels and negotiates numerous inclines along the route. With regular stations and halts, this gives passengers easy access to walks, tourist attractions and leisure opportunities at points along the line. A day on the East Lancashire Railway is never long enough, and repeat journeys are a must.

Special Event days are also a major feature throughout the year. With Santa Special trains, 1940s Wartime Weekends, Edwardian Trains, Halloween Specials, Teddy Bears Picnics, Classic Car events, Steam events, DMU days, Diesel Events; there is something to interest everyone. 2011 also sees the return of Days out with Thomas to appeal to younger visitors. The Bury Transport Museum is another attraction for visitors to Bury.

I really hope that you enjoy this book. I also hope that it inspires you to take a trip on the East Lancashire Railway and savour its delights for yourself.

LIST OF ILLUSTRATIONS

The East Lancashire Railway has its headquarters at Bury Bolton Street Station. The Preservation Trust manages to attract a wide variety of visiting locos each year. The year 2007 was no exception, with the visit of 4771 *Green Arrow* from the National Collection. The photograph is carefully framed to show the location.

A more regular visitor to the railway is LMS Jubilee 5690 *Leander,* seen here in platform 2 at Bury Bolton Street Station.

The first new steam locomotive to be built in the United Kingdom since 1960, A1 Pacific 60163 *Tornado*, was completed in 2008 and can be seen here in October 2010, about to depart from Bury on its first ever outing on a north-west preserved railway. Despite the persistent rain, large crowds turned out for this unique event.

To the east of Bury lies Heywood Station. This section of the line is not the most attractive, being predominantly industrial. The line does, however, pass over Roch Viaduct, an impressive seven-arched brick structure.

Heywood Station is the most recently opened station on the line. It also gives main-line access, allowing locomotive and stock easy access for interchange. It also offers the opportunity for locomotives to take on water as seen here. Trains occasionally run throughout the night on special weekends.

On a bright, crisp winter's morning, a long train is hauled across Roch Viaduct en route to Heywood.

After leaving Bury Bolton Street Station on the main section of the line, the railway passes through Burrs Country Park. Originally the site of a large mill, the remains of the waterwheel can be seen here.

Opposite: Burrs is probably the most popular photographic location on the line, as locomotives are made to work hard up the incline. This could be considered a typical Burrs image, with the blue sky and snow adding an extra sparkle.

Burrs is also an excellent location to get silhouetted images in front of a setting sun. On this occasion, the reflective quality of the snow allowed me to retain some detail in the foreground.

Autumn at Burrs. Rich colours glow in the sunlight, as LMS Jubilee *Leander* crosses the viaduct with a long train.

Between Burrs and Summerseat Station, the line curves through open countryside, farms and wooded areas, remaining attractive all the way to Ramsbottom.

The line continues to follow a series of curves on the approach to Summerseat.

Taken from the footpath crossing, this view of a double-headed train shows an unlikely pairing. While the second locomotive dates from the 1940s, the main engine is ex-Lancashire and Yorkshire Class 27 No. 1300, built in 1896.

Opposite: Immediately prior to Summerseat Station, the line passes through a wooded cutting. One of the Trust's many heritage diesels can be seen here, heading out of the station on a beautiful autumn day.

In BR days, the branch was double track. In preservation, the track was singled, and one of the original platforms was removed. The area where the second platform used to be has now been developed into attractive gardens by hard-working volunteers.

The whole valley creates an attractive backdrop at this location, as *Leander* departs with a train for Ramsbottom.

After leaving the station, the line passes over Brooksbottom Viaduct, an attractive stone and steel structure. The building visible in the background is a former cotton mill, now converted into a restaurant and flats.

The opposite view catches the morning light.

Having just returned to steam in late 2010, Black 5, 45337 crosses the viaduct.

Immediately after crossing the viaduct, trains enter Brooksbottom Tunnel.

Trains emerge from Brooksbottom Tunnel very briefly before entering Nuttal Tunnel. 47324 *Jinty* emerges from Nuttal Tunnel, belching steam and smoke on a bright, but very wet summer's day.

On the outskirts of Ramsbottom, trains pass through Nuttal Park, crossing the River Irwell on the edge of the park. The plate girder bridge is rather scruffy, but the scene becomes much more attractive with a covering of snow.

Ramsbottom is an attractive station, and even on a winter's day retains a welcoming look. Gresley K4 Mogul, *The Great Marquess* was a guest loco for the January 2010 BR steam event.

Being the central station on the line, Ramsbottom is twin track with two platforms, acting as the passing point for trains whenever the line is being operated by more than one train. On a diesel day Class 37 37518 passes Class 50 *Valiant*, heading for Rawtenstall.

During December, steam trains head Santa Specials between Bury and Ramsbottom. On this particular day, with temperatures dipping below -10 degrees, the Santa Special has arrived at Ramsbottom and is waiting for the shuttle from Rawtenstall to arrive with passengers for Bury.

Unfortunately, the level crossing gate mechanism had frozen solid, so passengers had to disembark from the DMU shuttle and walk along the line to join the Santa special. Maybe it was the wrong kind of snow on the line!

During a diesel event in March 2010, a night-rider service was offered, with all night running in the hands of Class 47 D1501.

After crossing the road via the level crossing, the line passes storage sidings and then starts to climb towards Stubbins, the site of a station on the line during BR days.

The same location looks very different when gripped by a deep winter freeze.

Opposite: After passing the sidings, the locomotives have to work hard up a steep incline on the approach to the old station. The vivid colours contrast with the plumes of smoke to create a striking image.

The previous image does not tell the whole story. The opposite view here shows the large Georgia Pacific factory complex that runs alongside the line at this point.

The line quickly becomes rural again, passing a small village as it works its way towards Irwell Vale. The train, headed by 50015 *Valiant*, gleams in the winter sunlight.

Originally, the line branched at Stubbins, with the main line heading across Higher Alderbottom Viaduct towards Accrington as both lines crossed the River Irwell. This is the view from beneath the viaduct.

Looking down from the Higher Alderbottom Viaduct gives a fine panoramic view, showing how densely wooded this area is. It also gives some indication of just how high this structure is.

At Irwell Vale, an attractive halt was built in preference to restoring the station at Ewood Bridge. The rural nature of the location is evident here.

Opposite: Austerity 0-6-0ST No. 15 *Earl David* makes a powerful departure from Irwell Vale.

During the winter months, trains are timetabled so that they do not stop at Irwell Vale during the hours of darkness. On this occasion, however, trains were running over half an hour late. The result is this very rare shot of a train departing from Irwell Vale well after sunset.

Between Irwell Vale and Ewood Bridge, the River Irwell is crossed twice. Black 5 44871 traverses the first of these crossings. You can clearly see how a new concrete bridge has been installed, incorporating the original stone piers.

A change of season as the bridge from the previous picture is crossed by a DMU from Rawtenstall.

Unique BR Class 8 Pacific No. 71000 *Duke of Gloucester* crosses the second of the new bridges on a glorious summer's day.

Class 33 D6525 heads through Ewood Bridge. The remains of the old station platform can be seen on the left.

The area around Ewood Bridge is mainly rural and very attractive. What you can't see in this picture is a large sewage works hidden behind the trees on the left.

Between Ewood Bridge and Rawtenstall, the line passes through Townsend Fold, skirting the river as the line briefly becomes rural at this point. An Ivatt Class 2 and the unique Class 8 Pacific, *Duke of Gloucester*, make an unusual pairing double heading the train.

The railway's terminus is at Rawtenstall, where the station is surrounded by large mills, reflecting the town's past. The station building has been built in the style of the original buildings on the line, making an impressive place to start or end your journey.

A famous visitor to Rawtenstall was GWR 3700 Class 3440 *City of Truro*, claimed to be the first steam locomotive to travel in excess of 100 mph during trials in 1904. It is now preserved as part of the national collection.

During a quiet moment the driver and guard of a class 101 DMU seem to be in deep discussion about the controls.

The East Lancashire Railway runs a large variety of special events. The following ten pages showcase a selection of these events. Classic car days are very popular, attracting large numbers of exhibits and visitors.

Gleaming classic cars line up in Bury Station car park with Pullman dining carriages behind.

On special event days, members of the public are given the opportunity to drive a tank engine up and down the sidings at Rawtenstall Station.

Catering for younger visitors, the ELR trust regularly runs 'Jimmy the Jinty and friends' weekends. Watched by crowds, *Gothenburg the tank engine* heads off to collect trucks from the sidings at Ramsbottom.

Children are also encouraged to get up close to visiting locomotives, even being allowed onto the footplate like this excited boy, my son Thomas, aged nine at the time.

Among the most popular special events each year are the 1940s wartime weekends. Irwell Vale becomes Ross-on-Vale and plays host to an American Army camp.

American troops at Rawtenstall wait for the train to depart before engaging German Axis Paratroopers.

Rawtenstall becomes rural France, as a resistance fighter distracts occupying German officers.

More images from the wartime weekend.

A selection of candid images from special event weekends.

Class 40 40145 and Class 33 37418 double head a train out of a snow-covered Rawtenstall on the return journey.

Black 5 44871 heads through Ewood Bridge, going towards Irwell Vale.

On a lovely winter's day, with clear blue skies, the River Irwell is crossed near Ewood Bridge.

Standard 4 tank 80072 approaches the first river crossing at Irwell Vale in February 2011. White smoke really stands out against the dark, brooding sky.

Class 55 Diesel 55022 *Royal Scots Grey* is preserved with main-line certification. As well as appearing regularly on the ELR it also sees use on a variety of rail tours. The year 2011 also sees 55022 celebrate its 50th birthday, with a number of events planned.

Opposite: On loan from the Great Central Railway, SR King Arthur Class 30777 *Sir Lamiel*, part of the national collection, heads through Irwell Vale in February 2010.

Reflecting the rural nature of Irwell Vale, this picture paints a halcyon image. With nothing modern to date it, this could easily be a photograph from the 1950s.

Opposite: 70013 approaches Irwell Vale with a train from Rawtenstall.

On a rare bright day in August 2010, the mismatched units on the DMU give it a rather quirky look as it trundles slowly through the Irwell Vale countryside.

Exuding power, Class 55 diesel 55022 heads from Irwell Vale to Stubbins during a special East Coast day.

The locomotive shunting the sidings at Ramsbottom is one of the smallest on the East Lancashire Railway. Locomotive 32 *Gothenberg* originally worked on the Manchester Ship Canal. This locomotive can also be seen wearing a smiley face as *Gothenberg the tank engine* on page 57.

A good overall view of Ramsbottom Station with a Class 122 pressed steel bubble car in platform 2.

The River Irwell is crossed in Nuttal Park, Ramsbottom.

The same bridge is crossed in very different conditions by a Santa Special in December 2009. The snow positively sparkles under bright blue skies.

On the East Lancashire Railway, locomotives are usually turned out facing Rawtenstall, making shots like this one fairly uncommon. 44871 bursts out of Brooksbottom Tunnel and approaches the viaduct.

Duke of Gloucester crosses Brooksbottom Viaduct, showing the opposite view to the one seen on page 24.

Class 101 DMU heads up through the cutting as it leaves Summerseat Station in November 2010.

Opposite: Late summer, same location. With the trees in full leaf, the cutting takes on a very different appearance. Earlier in the day, there was heavy rainfall, adding an extra sparkle to the scene under bright, sunlit conditions.

The weather was so bad on this day in December 2009 that the steam power originally planned had to be replaced by a Class 40, as the water towers were frozen and no water could be taken on. With deep snow all around, the blizzard conditions are clearly evident.

Once through the wooded area at Summerseat, the line passes farmland as it approaches Burrs. With a covering of snow, the setting is perfect for a Santa Special in December 2010.

With cows in the fields around Burrs, the railway looks every part the idyllic rural branch line. Only the train disturbs the peace.

Taken from a higher position than the previous photograph, the true character of this area becomes apparent, with a caravan park on the far side of the line. Future plans for this area include extending the caravan park and providing a halt to serve the area.

Caprotti Standard 5 No. 73129 works hard up the incline creating a typical Burrs shot. This viewpoint will soon be a thing of the past as this field is due to become part of the caravan park.

No. 80080 gleams in the early spring sunshine at Burrs.

Tornado attracts the attention of a couple of wildlife enthusiasts as it crosses the viaduct in Burrs Country Park.

One of the smaller locos to visit the ELR is No. 30587, a Beattie Well Tank 2-4-0WT, seen here at Bury Station in 2007. Built in 1874, this tiny loco still sees regular service on the Bodmin and Wenford railway.

Standard Class 4 No. 80072 arrives at Bury Bolton Street with a train from Heywood, passing a waiting freight train. This picture shows the layout of the station with platform access via stairs from the road-level footbridge.

The Locomotive Department is located at Buckley Wells, Bury. Facilities include a large steam locomotive shed plus workshops. This is also an excellent location for night-time photography under the floodlights during enthusiast weekends.

There is often the opportunity to photograph some very impressive visiting locos. Class 7, 70013 *Oliver Cromwell* worked the last steam rail tour on BR in 1968. It is now part of the national collection.

Class 55 Deltic *Gordon Highlander* also looks impressive under the floodlights.

The future of the railway seems assured. Future expansion plans combined with the large number of families visiting the line suggest that the East Lancashire Railway will continue to be a significant tourist attraction in the north-west. This timeless image was taken by my twelve-year-old son, Thomas; another sign that the railway will be supported for many years to come.

Opposite: Another atmospheric shot, particularly with some natural light retained in the sky.

AUTHOR'S NOTES

I am a full time teacher of Design and Technology at Sir John Thursby Community College, Burnley. My interest in photography complements the teaching of graphic design, benefitting both areas of my life.

   This book combines two of my main interests, namely photography and transport. My interest in railways was developed at a young age, as can be seen from the picture of me aged eighteen months at Rosegrove engine sheds during the last days of steam. This has developed over the years, culminating in this, my first book.